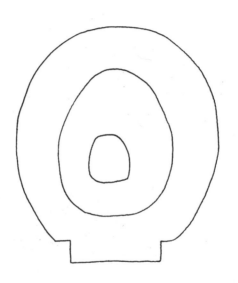

Poo Log

A Record Keeper

By Josh Richman and
Anish Sheth, M.D.

Illustrations by Peter Arkle

CHRONICLE BOOKS
SAN FRANCISCO

ISBN 978-0-8118-6339-1

Manufactured in China
Designed by Jacob T. Gardner
Typeset in Cooper Black and New Century Schoolbook

Chronicle Books endeavors to use environmentally
responsible paper in its gift and stationery products.

10 9 8 7 6 5 4 3 2 1

Chronicle Books LLC
680 Second Street
San Francisco, CA 94107
www.chroniclebooks.com

Introduction

Let's face it. There is no substitute for the hard (hopefully, not *too* hard) facts.

We track our financial well-being by keeping an eye on our stock portfolios, monitor our cardiovascular health by checking our cholesterol, and even assess our popularity by the number of hits to our personal Web sites (check out ours, www.dr stool.com).

But unfortunately, instead of being thoroughly evaluated, poo has aimlessly floated through history having escaped objective analysis. It is too often hastily disposed of and rendered as a useless and malodorous waste product. Rather than embracing poo's power to teach us about our gastrointestinal health, millennia of humans have simply turned the other cheek.

Until now, there has been no metric by which you could scientifically evaluate your stool. But this log book will change all of that! It is now time to free poo from its place in the societal outhouse and give it the attention it deserves. This log book's newly created Poo Quality Index, or PQI, will allow you to record salient characteristics of your daily deed with the utmost precision. (In initial beta testing, most satisfying poos registered scores of 10 or higher.) Furthermore, this numerical scale will offer a standardized means by which to continue the evolving discourse of poo. No longer will one man's Monster Poo be another's Pebble Poo. . . .

So get ready, it's time to keep score in this game of craps. Whether you keep this log for yourself or share it with your friends and family, use it early and use it often.

There is a new bottom line when it comes to your poo — so look before you flush and keep a log!

Glossary of Poo

Camouflage Poo

Synonyms: *Dalmatian Dookie, Chocolate Chip Cookie Doo, Black and Tan, Olive Loaf*

Characteristics: Multitoned poo (varying shades of black, brown, and green); looks like a mosaic of different excrement from different sources and from different meals; texture is usually bumpy

The Chinese Star

Synonyms: *The Dorito, Iceberg, Glass Shard, Mystery Poo*

Characteristics: Particularly hard and angular-shaped; excruciatingly painful sensation of feeling as if your rectum is being torn apart from the inside as this type of poo exits your body

The Clean Sweep

Synonyms: *Wipeless Poo, The Perfect Wipe, Mr. Clean*

Characteristics: In the cleanup phase there is no poo residue on the toilet paper; some experts consider the "wipeless" poo to be the pinnacle of poo performance

Curtain Call

Synonyms: *Overtime, Bonus Baby, Groundhog Day, The Remix*

Characteristics: You finish defecating, wipe, pull up your pants, flush the toilet, and suddenly feel a stomach grumble; your GI tract is ostensibly ringing the bell for Round 2 and it's time to get back in the ring

D.A.D.S. (a.k.a. "Day-After-Drinking Stool")
Synonyms: *Revenge of the Poo, Morning After, Poo of Shame, Bud Mud*
Characteristics: Often comes in a semisolid state, and sometimes is accompanied by stomach discomfort; most notable trait is the tread mark left on the toilet bowl after flushing, as well as the distinctive bar-floor smell

Déjà Poo
Synonyms: *Veggie Burger, Leftovers, Corn-Backed Rattler, Sloppy Seconds*
Characteristics: Has remarkably familiar portions of a recent meal embedded in it; can include a potpourri of colors, often containing pieces of vegetables (most notoriously corn)

Dunce Cap
Synonyms: *Conehead, Cylinder Poo, Tapered Wafer, Biggie Small*
Characteristics: Begins with a thick base but then scales down to a point

Gift Poo
Synonyms: *Pollyanna Poo, Phantom Poo, Surprise Party, Shock and Awe, Flushless Folly, River Pickle*
Characteristics: Dump left behind in toilets without flushing; comes in all shapes and sizes and is most prevalent in public restrooms and fraternity houses

The Green Goblin
Synonym: *Seaweed Stool*
Characteristics: Thankfully rare, an explosion of foul-smelling diarrhea that is characterized by its viridian hue; deep-set, blackish-green appearance

Hanging Chad

Synonyms: *Grundle Weeds, Cling-Ons, Butt Bark, The Lone Ranger, Crap Crumbs*

Characteristics: Stubborn pieces of turd that cling to the anal hairs and often refuse to let go

Log Jam

Synonyms: *Can't Get the Train Out of the Tunnel, Colon Congestion, Corked, F.O.S., Stuck Up, Crying Wolf, False Alarm*

Characteristics: Even worse than Pebble Poo is no poo at all; despite stomach pains, rancid gas, and feeling a turd on deck, nothing comes out, no matter how hard you try to push

Monster Poo

Synonyms: *Lincoln Log, The Crowd-Pleaser, Double Deuce, The Five-Minute Diet*

Characteristics: Massive girth; tendency to extend from the bottom of the toilet bowl beyond the water surface; not always easy to discharge; great feeling of accomplishment and pride associated with the deposit of a Monster Poo

Number Three

Synonyms: *Butt Piss, Liquid Poo, The Runs, Oil Spill, Hershey Squirts, Deuce Juice, Rectum Rapids*

Characteristics: Comes in a liquid form; feels as if urinating out of the wrong side; often a violent discharge, sometimes with very little warning

Pebble Poo

Synonyms: *Rabbit Poo, Kibbles'n'Bits, Splashers, Butt Hail, Blueberries, Buckshot, Meteor Shower*

Characteristics: Small, hard, disjointed poos; leaves you unsatisfied and unfulfilled

Poo-phoria

Synonyms: *Holy Crap, Mood Enhancer, The Tingler*

Characteristics: Large in volume but varying in form; distinguished by the sense of euphoria and ecstasy that you feel throughout your body when this type of feces departs your system; often accompanied by goose bumps and even a little light-headedness

Rambo Poo

Synonyms: *Uh-Oh, Chocolate Sundae with Strawberry Sauce, The Neapolitan Poo*

Characteristics: Traces of blood found on poo or on toilet paper

Ring of Fire

Synonyms: *Acid Poo, Hooters Souvenir, Curry in a Hurry, Fire in the Hole, Tabasco Turd, Feeling the Burn*

Characteristics: Burning sensation rips through anus and as every millimeter of poo passes through you, the burning only gets more excruciating

The Ritual Poo

Synonyms: *Rite of Passage, Palm Poo, Calendar Crap*

Characteristics: Occurs at the same time each day; the regularity of these poos may provide comfort in an otherwise unpredictable world

Rotten Poo

Synonyms: *Napalm, Rancid Poo, Aftershock Poo, Agent Orange*
Characteristics: Distinguishing feature is its atrocious and unbearable odor; odor will linger and may promptly cause you and others to experience severe gagging and nausea

The Snake

Synonyms: *Curly Fry, The Long Thin Line, Fettuccine Feces*
Characteristics: Thin and windy; can contort itself into a variety of different shapes and sizes; regardless of the final form, seems to go on forever as it leaves your rectum

Sneak Attack

Synonyms: *Ambush Poo, Chocolate Surprise, Deuce Is Loose, Shart*
Characteristics: Usually starts with the uncomfortable sensations of intestinal rumbling and gaseous bloating; the anticipated fart contains more than just gas and is accompanied by a liquid smear of poo

Soft Serve

Synonyms: *Jabba the Poo, Play Doo, Cow Pattie, Septic Seepage*
Characteristics: More dense than diarrhea but softer than a normal poo, this solid yet amorphous turd comes out in one smooth, steady flowing motion

The Streak

Synonyms: *Skidmark, Hershey Highway, Racing Stripe, Lining the Pavement*
Characteristics: Relic of a prior poo usually appearing as a thin brown stain down the center of the toilet bowl; appears only after completion of the flush

Poo Quality Index (PQI):

	1	2	3	Score
Delivery	Epidural, please!	Couple of pushes, no grunts	Smooth like butter, baby	
Size/Shape	Pebble Poo **OR** Liquid	Snake-like girth **OR** stubby	Monster Poo; stool breaks water surface	
Number of particles	More than two	Two, The Deuce	One and done, baby!	
Smell	Vomit-inducing	Mildly odoriferous	Odorless	
Number of wipes	Another roll, please!	More than one	One (no stool on paper)	
Post-poo sentiment	Woulda, coulda, shoulda	Satisfaction	Poo-phoria	
			TOTAL	

Name: _____

Date: _____ - _____ - _____   Time: _____ : _____ ☐ AM ☐ PM

Duration: _____

Unusual Characteristics: _____

_____

_____

_____

Sketch:

```
┌─ ─ ─ ─ ─ ─ ─ ─ ─ ─ ─ ─ ─ ─ ─ ─ ─ ─ ┐
│                                     │
│                                     │
│                                     │
│                                     │
│                                     │
│                                     │
│                                     │
└─ ─ ─ ─ ─ ─ ─ ─ ─ ─ ─ ─ ─ ─ ─ ─ ─ ─ ┘
```

Doo You Know? A recent study showed that, while 95 percent of men and women surveyed say they wash their hands after using a public restroom, only 67 percent of people actually do.

Poo Quality Index (PQI):

	1	2	3	Score
Delivery	Epidural, please!	Couple of pushes, no grunts	Smooth like butter, baby	
Size/Shape	Pebble Poo **OR** Liquid	Snake-like girth **OR** stubby	Monster Poo; stool breaks water surface	
Number of particles	More than two	Two, The Deuce	One and done, baby!	
Smell	Vomit-inducing	Mildly odoriferous	Odorless	
Number of wipes	Another roll, please!	More than one	One (no stool on paper)	
Post-poo sentiment	Woulda, coulda, shoulda	Satisfaction	Poo-phoria	
			TOTAL	

Name:

Date: -   -   Time: :   ☐ AM ☐ PM

Duration:

Unusual Characteristics:

Sketch:

Doo You Know? The average person farts ten times per day, resulting in the release of 705 cc of gas into the atmosphere.

Poo Quality Index (PQI):

	1	2	3	Score
Delivery	Epidural, please!	Couple of pushes, no grunts	Smooth like butter, baby	
Size/Shape	Pebble Poo **OR** Liquid	Snake-like girth **OR** stubby	Monster Poo; stool breaks water surface	
Number of particles	More than two	Two, The Deuce	One and done, baby!	
Smell	Vomit-inducing	Mildly odoriferous	Odorless	
Number of wipes	Another roll, please!	More than one	One (no stool on paper)	
Post-poo sentiment	Woulda, coulda, shoulda	Satisfaction	Poo-phoria	
			TOTAL	

Name:

Date: -   -

Time: :   ☐ AM ☐ PM

Duration:

Unusual Characteristics:

Sketch:

Doo You Know? The average weight of stool excreted per day is 450 grams (about a pound).

Poo Quality Index (PQI):

	1	2	3	Score
Delivery	Epidural, please!	Couple of pushes, no grunts	Smooth like butter, baby	
Size/Shape	Pebble Poo **OR** Liquid	Snake-like girth **OR** stubby	Monster Poo; stool breaks water surface	
Number of particles	More than two	Two, The Deuce	One and done, baby!	
Smell	Vomit-inducing	Mildly odoriferous	Odorless	
Number of wipes	Another roll, please!	More than one	One (no stool on paper)	
Post-poo sentiment	Woulda, coulda, shoulda	Satisfaction	Poo-phoria	
			TOTAL	

Name: _____

Date: ____ - ____ - ____   Time: ____ : ____ ☐ AM ☐ PM

Duration: _____

Unusual Characteristics: _____

_____

_____

_____

Sketch:

Doo You Know? The amount of stool expelled per day varies from country to country. The average weight of stool in England is 106 grams/day, while South Asians unload nearly three times that amount. This difference is largely due to the higher fiber content in the average Indian diet.

Poo Quality Index (PQI):

	1	2	3	Score
Delivery	Epidural, please!	Couple of pushes, no grunts	Smooth like butter, baby	
Size/Shape	Pebble Poo **OR** Liquid	Snake-like girth **OR** stubby	Monster Poo; stool breaks water surface	
Number of particles	More than two	Two, The Deuce	One and done, baby!	
Smell	Vomit-inducing	Mildly odoriferous	Odorless	
Number of wipes	Another roll, please!	More than one	One (no stool on paper)	
Post-poo sentiment	Woulda, coulda, shoulda	Satisfaction	Poo-phoria	
			TOTAL	

Name: _____

Date: _____ - ___ - ___   Time: ___ : ___ ☐ AM ☐ PM

Duration: _____

Unusual Characteristics: _____

_____

_____

_____

Sketch:

```
┌ ─ ─ ─ ─ ─ ─ ─ ─ ─ ─ ─ ─ ─ ─ ─ ─ ─ ─ ─ ┐
│                                         │
│                                         │
│                                         │
│                                         │
│                                         │
│                                         │
│                                         │
│                                         │
│                                         │
│                                         │
└ ─ ─ ─ ─ ─ ─ ─ ─ ─ ─ ─ ─ ─ ─ ─ ─ ─ ─ ─ ┘
```

Doo You Know? Studies of healthy subjects have revealed a wide variation in stool frequency. The current accepted range for "normal" is from three bowel movements per day to three bowel movements per week.

Poo Quality Index (PQI):

	1	2	3	Score
Delivery	Epidural, please!	Couple of pushes, no grunts	Smooth like butter, baby	
Size/Shape	Pebble Poo **OR** Liquid	Snake-like girth **OR** stubby	Monster Poo; stool breaks water surface	
Number of particles	More than two	Two, The Deuce	One and done, baby!	
Smell	Vomit-inducing	Mildly odoriferous	Odorless	
Number of wipes	Another roll, please!	More than one	One (no stool on paper)	
Post-poo sentiment	Woulda, coulda, shoulda	Satisfaction	Poo-phoria	
			TOTAL	

Name: _____

Date: _____ - _____ - _____   Time: _____ : _____ ☐ AM ☐ PM

Duration: _____

Unusual Characteristics: _____

_____

_____

_____

Sketch:

Doo You Know? What's Poo Made Of? •10 parts water •1 part bacteria (dead and alive) •1 part indigestible fiber •1 part mixture of fat, protein, dead cells, mucus

Poo Quality Index (PQI):

	1	2	3	Score
Delivery	Epidural, please!	Couple of pushes, no grunts	Smooth like butter, baby	
Size/Shape	Pebble Poo **OR** Liquid	Snake-like girth **OR** stubby	Monster Poo; stool breaks water surface	
Number of particles	More than two	Two, The Deuce	One and done, baby!	
Smell	Vomit-inducing	Mildly odoriferous	Odorless	
Number of wipes	Another roll, please!	More than one	One (no stool on paper)	
Post-poo sentiment	Woulda, coulda, shoulda	Satisfaction	Poo-phoria	
			TOTAL	

Name:

Date: - -   Time: : ☐ AM ☐ PM

Duration:

Unusual Characteristics:

Sketch:

Doo You Know? •Rabbits can produce over 500 pellets of poo every day. •Horses poo ten pounds worth of dung, often without breaking stride. •Geese poo, on average, once every twelve minutes. •Bears don't poo at all when hibernating. Their bodies create an internal plug made from feces and hair that prevents them from pooping while sleeping.

Poo Quality Index (PQI):

	1	2	3	Score
Delivery	Epidural, please!	Couple of pushes, no grunts	Smooth like butter, baby	
Size/Shape	Pebble Poo **OR** Liquid	Snake-like girth **OR** stubby	Monster Poo; stool breaks water surface	
Number of particles	More than two	Two, The Deuce	One and done, baby!	
Smell	Vomit-inducing	Mildly odoriferous	Odorless	
Number of wipes	Another roll, please!	More than one	One (no stool on paper)	
Post-poo sentiment	Woulda, coulda, shoulda	Satisfaction	Poo-phoria	
			TOTAL	

Name: _____

Date: _____ - _____ - _____   Time: _____ : _____ ☐ AM ☐ PM

Duration: _____

Unusual Characteristics: _____

_____

_____

_____

Sketch:

Doo You Know? **Foods That Cause Gas:** •Beans •Vegetables, such as broccoli, cabbage, brussels sprouts, onions, artichokes, and asparagus •Fruits, such as pears, apples, and peaches •Whole grains •Soft drinks •Milk •Sorbitol (used as a sugar substitute in diet foods

Poo Quality Index (PQI):

	1	2	3	Score
Delivery	Epidural, please!	Couple of pushes, no grunts	Smooth like butter, baby	
Size/Shape	Pebble Poo **OR** Liquid	Snake-like girth **OR** stubby	Monster Poo; stool breaks water surface	
Number of particles	More than two	Two, The Deuce	One and done, baby!	
Smell	Vomit-inducing	Mildly odoriferous	Odorless	
Number of wipes	Another roll, please!	More than one	One (no stool on paper)	
Post-poo sentiment	Woulda, coulda, shoulda	Satisfaction	Poo-phoria	
			TOTAL	

Name: _____

Date: _____ - _____ - _____   Time: _____ : _____ ☐ AM ☐ PM

Duration: _____

Unusual Characteristics: _____

_____

_____

_____

Sketch:

```
┌ ─ ─ ─ ─ ─ ─ ─ ─ ─ ─ ─ ─ ─ ─ ─ ─ ─ ─ ┐
│                                      │
│                                      │
│                                      │
│                                      │
│                                      │
│                                      │
│                                      │
│                                      │
│                                      │
│                                      │
│                                      │
└ ─ ─ ─ ─ ─ ─ ─ ─ ─ ─ ─ ─ ─ ─ ─ ─ ─ ─ ┘
```

Doo You Know? A recent study showed that, while 95 percent of men and women surveyed say they wash their hands after using a public restroom, only 67 percent of people actually do.

Poo Quality Index (PQI):

	1	2	3	Score
Delivery	Epidural, please!	Couple of pushes, no grunts	Smooth like butter, baby	
Size/Shape	Pebble Poo **OR** Liquid	Snake-like girth **OR** stubby	Monster Poo; stool breaks water surface	
Number of particles	More than two	Two, The Deuce	One and done, baby!	
Smell	Vomit-inducing	Mildly odoriferous	Odorless	
Number of wipes	Another roll, please!	More than one	One (no stool on paper)	
Post-poo sentiment	Woulda, coulda, shoulda	Satisfaction	Poo-phoria	
			TOTAL	

Name: _____

Date: _____ - ___ - ___   Time: ____ : ___ ☐ AM ☐ PM

Duration: _____

Unusual Characteristics: _____

_____

_____

_____

Sketch:

```
┌ ─ ─ ─ ─ ─ ─ ─ ─ ─ ─ ─ ─ ─ ─ ─ ─ ─ ─ ─ ─ ┐
│                                          │
│                                          │
│                                          │
│                                          │
│                                          │
│                                          │
│                                          │
│                                          │
│                                          │
└ ─ ─ ─ ─ ─ ─ ─ ─ ─ ─ ─ ─ ─ ─ ─ ─ ─ ─ ─ ─ ┘
```

Doo You Know? The average person farts ten times per day, resulting in the release of 705 cc of gas into the atmosphere.

Poo Quality Index (PQI):

	1	2	3	Score
Delivery	Epidural, please!	Couple of pushes, no grunts	Smooth like butter, baby	
Size/Shape	Pebble Poo **OR** Liquid	Snake-like girth **OR** stubby	Monster Poo; stool breaks water surface	
Number of particles	More than two	Two, The Deuce	One and done, baby!	
Smell	Vomit-inducing	Mildly odoriferous	Odorless	
Number of wipes	Another roll, please!	More than one	One (no stool on paper)	
Post-poo sentiment	Woulda, coulda, shoulda	Satisfaction	Poo-phoria	
			TOTAL	

Name: _____

Date: _____ - _____ - _____   Time: _____ : _____ ☐ AM ☐ PM

Duration: _____

Unusual Characteristics: _____

_____

_____

_____

Sketch:

```
┌ ─ ─ ─ ─ ─ ─ ─ ─ ─ ─ ─ ─ ─ ─ ─ ─ ─ ─ ─ ─ ─ ─ ┐
│                                              │
│                                              │
│                                              │
│                                              │
│                                              │
│                                              │
│                                              │
└ ─ ─ ─ ─ ─ ─ ─ ─ ─ ─ ─ ─ ─ ─ ─ ─ ─ ─ ─ ─ ─ ─ ┘
```

Doo You Know? The average weight of stool excreted per day is 450 grams (about a pound).

Poo Quality Index (PQI):

	1	2	3	Score
Delivery	Epidural, please!	Couple of pushes, no grunts	Smooth like butter, baby	
Size/Shape	Pebble Poo **OR** Liquid	Snake-like girth **OR** stubby	Monster Poo; stool breaks water surface	
Number of particles	More than two	Two, The Deuce	One and done, baby!	
Smell	Vomit-inducing	Mildly odoriferous	Odorless	
Number of wipes	Another roll, please!	More than one	One (no stool on paper)	
Post-poo sentiment	Woulda, coulda, shoulda	Satisfaction	Poo-phoria	
			TOTAL	

Name: _____

Date: _____ - _____ - _____   Time: _____ : _____ ☐ AM ☐ PM

Duration: _____

Unusual Characteristics: _____

_____

_____

_____

Sketch:

Doo You Know? The amount of stool expelled per day varies from country to country. The average weight of stool in England is 106 grams/day, while South Asians unload nearly three times that amount. This difference is largely due to the higher fiber content in the average Indian diet.

Poo Quality Index (PQI):

	1	2	3	Score
Delivery	Epidural, please!	Couple of pushes, no grunts	Smooth like butter, baby	
Size/Shape	Pebble Poo **OR** Liquid	Snake-like girth **OR** stubby	Monster Poo; stool breaks water surface	
Number of particles	More than two	Two, The Deuce	One and done, baby!	
Smell	Vomit-inducing	Mildly odoriferous	Odorless	
Number of wipes	Another roll, please!	More than one	One (no stool on paper)	
Post-poo sentiment	Woulda, coulda, shoulda	Satisfaction	Poo-phoria	
			TOTAL	

Name: _____

Date: _____ - ___ - ___   Time: _____ : ____ ☐ AM ☐ PM

Duration: _____

Unusual Characteristics: _____

_____

_____

_____

Sketch:

```
┌ ─ ─ ─ ─ ─ ─ ─ ─ ─ ─ ─ ─ ─ ─ ─ ─ ─ ─ ┐
│                                     │
│                                     │
│                                     │
│                                     │
│                                     │
│                                     │
│                                     │
│                                     │
│                                     │
│                                     │
└ ─ ─ ─ ─ ─ ─ ─ ─ ─ ─ ─ ─ ─ ─ ─ ─ ─ ─ ┘
```

Doo You Know? Studies of healthy subjects have revealed a wide variation in stool frequency. The current accepted range for "normal" is from three bowel movements per day to three bowel movements per week.

Poo Quality Index (PQI):

	1	2	3	Score
Delivery	Epidural, please!	Couple of pushes, no grunts	Smooth like butter, baby	
Size/Shape	Pebble Poo **OR** Liquid	Snake-like girth **OR** stubby	Monster Poo; stool breaks water surface	
Number of particles	More than two	Two, The Deuce	One and done, baby!	
Smell	Vomit-inducing	Mildly odoriferous	Odorless	
Number of wipes	Another roll, please!	More than one	One (no stool on paper)	
Post-poo sentiment	Woulda, coulda, shoulda	Satisfaction	Poo-phoria	
			TOTAL	

Name: _____

Date: _____ - _____ - _____   Time: _____ : _____ ☐ AM ☐ PM

Duration: _____

Unusual Characteristics: _____

_____

_____

_____

Sketch:

```
┌ ─ ─ ─ ─ ─ ─ ─ ─ ─ ─ ─ ─ ─ ─ ─ ─ ─ ─ ─ ─ ┐
│                                           │
│                                           │
│                                           │
│                                           │
│                                           │
│                                           │
│                                           │
│                                           │
│                                           │
│                                           │
└ ─ ─ ─ ─ ─ ─ ─ ─ ─ ─ ─ ─ ─ ─ ─ ─ ─ ─ ─ ─ ┘
```

Doo You Know? **What's Poo Made Of?** • 10 parts water • 1 part bacteria (dead and alive) • 1 part indigestible fiber • 1 part mixture of fat, protein, dead cells, mucus

Poo Quality Index (PQI):

	1	2	3	Score
Delivery	Epidural, please!	Couple of pushes, no grunts	Smooth like butter, baby	
Size/Shape	Pebble Poo **OR** Liquid	Snake-like girth **OR** stubby	Monster Poo; stool breaks water surface	
Number of particles	More than two	Two, The Deuce	One and done, baby!	
Smell	Vomit-inducing	Mildly odoriferous	Odorless	
Number of wipes	Another roll, please!	More than one	One (no stool on paper)	
Post-poo sentiment	Woulda, coulda, shoulda	Satisfaction	Poo-phoria	
			TOTAL	

Name: _____

Date: _____ - _____ - _____   Time: _____ : _____ ☐ AM ☐ PM

Duration: _____

Unusual Characteristics: _____

_____

_____

_____

Sketch:

Doo You Know? •Rabbits can produce over 500 pellets of poo every day. •Horses poo ten pounds worth of dung, often without breaking stride. •Geese poo, on average, once every twelve minutes. •Bears don't poo at all when hibernating. Their bodies create an internal plug made from feces and hair that prevents them from pooping while sleeping.

Poo Quality Index (PQI):

	1	2	3	Score
Delivery	Epidural, please!	Couple of pushes, no grunts	Smooth like butter, baby	
Size/Shape	Pebble Poo **OR** Liquid	Snake-like girth **OR** stubby	Monster Poo; stool breaks water surface	
Number of particles	More than two	Two, The Deuce	One and done, baby!	
Smell	Vomit-inducing	Mildly odoriferous	Odorless	
Number of wipes	Another roll, please!	More than one	One (no stool on paper)	
Post-poo sentiment	Woulda, coulda, shoulda	Satisfaction	Poo-phoria	
			TOTAL	

Name: _____

Date: ____ - __ - __   Time: ___ : ___ ☐ AM ☐ PM

Duration: _____

Unusual Characteristics: _____

_____

_____

_____

Sketch:

Poo Quality Index (PQI):

	1	2	3	Score
Delivery	Epidural, please!	Couple of pushes, no grunts	Smooth like butter, baby	
Size/Shape	Pebble Poo **OR** Liquid	Snake-like girth **OR** stubby	Monster Poo; stool breaks water surface	
Number of particles	More than two	Two, The Deuce	One and done, baby!	
Smell	Vomit-inducing	Mildly odoriferous	Odorless	
Number of wipes	Another roll, please!	More than one	One (no stool on paper)	
Post-poo sentiment	Woulda, coulda, shoulda	Satisfaction	Poo-phoria	
			TOTAL	

Name: _____

Date: _____ - _____ - _____   Time: _____ : _____ ☐ AM ☐ PM

Duration: _____

Unusual Characteristics: _____

_____

_____

_____

Sketch:

Doo You Know? A recent study showed that, while 95 percent of men and women surveyed say they wash their hands after using a public restroom, only 67 percent of people actually do.

Poo Quality Index (PQI):

	1	2	3	Score
Delivery	Epidural, please!	Couple of pushes, no grunts	Smooth like butter, baby	
Size/Shape	Pebble Poo **OR** Liquid	Snake-like girth **OR** stubby	Monster Poo; stool breaks water surface	
Number of particles	More than two	Two, The Deuce	One and done, baby!	
Smell	Vomit-inducing	Mildly odoriferous	Odorless	
Number of wipes	Another roll, please!	More than one	One (no stool on paper)	
Post-poo sentiment	Woulda, coulda, shoulda	Satisfaction	Poo-phoria	
			TOTAL	

Name: _____

Date: _____ - ___ - ___   Time: ___ : ___ ☐ AM ☐ PM

Duration: _____

Unusual Characteristics: _____

_____

_____

_____

Sketch:

Doo You Know? The average person farts ten times per day, resulting in the release of 705 cc of gas into the atmosphere.

Poo Quality Index (PQI):

	1	2	3	Score
Delivery	Epidural, please!	Couple of pushes, no grunts	Smooth like butter, baby	
Size/Shape	Pebble Poo **OR** Liquid	Snake-like girth **OR** stubby	Monster Poo; stool breaks water surface	
Number of particles	More than two	Two, The Deuce	One and done, baby!	
Smell	Vomit-inducing	Mildly odoriferous	Odorless	
Number of wipes	Another roll, please!	More than one	One (no stool on paper)	
Post-poo sentiment	Woulda, coulda, shoulda	Satisfaction	Poo-phoria	
			TOTAL	

Name: _____

Date: ___ - ___ - ___   Time: ___ : ___ ☐ AM ☐ PM

Duration: _____

Unusual Characteristics: _____
_____
_____
_____

Sketch:

```
┌ ─ ─ ─ ─ ─ ─ ─ ─ ─ ─ ─ ─ ─ ─ ─ ─ ─ ─ ─ ┐
│                                         │
│                                         │
│                                         │
│                                         │
│                                         │
│                                         │
│                                         │
└ ─ ─ ─ ─ ─ ─ ─ ─ ─ ─ ─ ─ ─ ─ ─ ─ ─ ─ ─ ┘
```

Doo You Know? The average weight of stool excreted per day is 450 grams (about a pound).

Poo Quality Index (PQI):

	1	2	3	Score
Delivery	Epidural, please!	Couple of pushes, no grunts	Smooth like butter, baby	
Size/Shape	Pebble Poo **OR** Liquid	Snake-like girth **OR** stubby	Monster Poo; stool breaks water surface	
Number of particles	More than two	Two, The Deuce	One and done, baby!	
Smell	Vomit-inducing	Mildly odoriferous	Odorless	
Number of wipes	Another roll, please!	More than one	One (no stool on paper)	
Post-poo sentiment	Woulda, coulda, shoulda	Satisfaction	Poo-phoria	
			TOTAL	

Name: _____

Date: ___ - _ - _   Time: __ : __ ☐ AM ☐ PM

Duration: _____

Unusual Characteristics: _____

_____

_____

_____

Sketch:

Doo You Know? The amount of stool expelled per day varies from country to country. The average weight of stool in England is 106 grams/day, while South Asians unload nearly three times that amount. This difference is largely due to the higher fiber content in the average Indian diet.

Poo Quality Index (PQI):

	1	2	3	Score
Delivery	Epidural, please!	Couple of pushes, no grunts	Smooth like butter, baby	
Size/Shape	Pebble Poo **OR** Liquid	Snake-like girth **OR** stubby	Monster Poo; stool breaks water surface	
Number of particles	More than two	Two, The Deuce	One and done, baby!	
Smell	Vomit-inducing	Mildly odoriferous	Odorless	
Number of wipes	Another roll, please!	More than one	One (no stool on paper)	
Post-poo sentiment	Woulda, coulda, shoulda	Satisfaction	Poo-phoria	
			TOTAL	

Name: _____

Date: ___ - ___ - ___   Time: ___ : ___ ☐ AM ☐ PM

Duration: _____

Unusual Characteristics: _____

_____

_____

_____

Sketch:

```
┌ ─ ─ ─ ─ ─ ─ ─ ─ ─ ─ ─ ─ ─ ─ ─ ─ ─ ─ ─ ─ ─ ┐
│                                             │
│                                             │
│                                             │
│                                             │
│                                             │
│                                             │
│                                             │
│                                             │
└ ─ ─ ─ ─ ─ ─ ─ ─ ─ ─ ─ ─ ─ ─ ─ ─ ─ ─ ─ ─ ─ ┘
```

Doo You Know? Studies of healthy subjects have revealed a wide variation in stool frequency. The current accepted range for "normal" is from three bowel movements per day to three bowel movements per week.

Poo Quality Index (PQI):

	1	2	3	Score
Delivery	Epidural, please!	Couple of pushes, no grunts	Smooth like butter, baby	
Size/Shape	Pebble Poo **OR** Liquid	Snake-like girth **OR** stubby	Monster Poo; stool breaks water surface	
Number of particles	More than two	Two, The Deuce	One and done, baby!	
Smell	Vomit-inducing	Mildly odoriferous	Odorless	
Number of wipes	Another roll, please!	More than one	One (no stool on paper)	
Post-poo sentiment	Woulda, coulda, shoulda	Satisfaction	Poo-phoria	
			TOTAL	

Name: _____

Date: _____ - ____ - ____   Time: _____ : _____ ☐ AM ☐ PM

Duration: _____

Unusual Characteristics: _____
_____
_____
_____

Sketch:

Doo You Know? **What's Poo Made Of?** • 10 parts water • 1 part bacteria (dead and alive) • 1 part indigestible fiber • 1 part mixture of fat, protein, dead cells, mucus

Poo Quality Index (PQI):

	1	2	3	Score
Delivery	Epidural, please!	Couple of pushes, no grunts	Smooth like butter, baby	
Size/Shape	Pebble Poo **OR** Liquid	Snake-like girth **OR** stubby	Monster Poo; stool breaks water surface	
Number of particles	More than two	Two, The Deuce	One and done, baby!	
Smell	Vomit-inducing	Mildly odoriferous	Odorless	
Number of wipes	Another roll, please!	More than one	One (no stool on paper)	
Post-poo sentiment	Woulda, coulda, shoulda	Satisfaction	Poo-phoria	
			TOTAL	

Name: _____

Date: ___ - ___ - ___   Time: ___ : ___ ☐ AM ☐ PM

Duration: _____

Unusual Characteristics: _____

_____

_____

_____

Sketch:

```
┌─────────────────────────────────────┐
│                                     │
│                                     │
│                                     │
│                                     │
│                                     │
│                                     │
│                                     │
│                                     │
└─────────────────────────────────────┘
```

Doo You Know? **Foods That Cause Gas:** •Beans •Vegetables, such as broccoli, cabbage, brussels sprouts, onions, artichokes, and asparagus •Fruits, such as pears, apples, and peaches •Whole grains •Soft drinks •Milk •Sorbitol (used as a sugar substitute in diet foods

Poo Quality Index (PQI):

	1	2	3	Score
Delivery	Epidural, please!	Couple of pushes, no grunts	Smooth like butter, baby	
Size/Shape	Pebble Poo **OR** Liquid	Snake-like girth **OR** stubby	Monster Poo; stool breaks water surface	
Number of particles	More than two	Two, The Deuce	One and done, baby!	
Smell	Vomit-inducing	Mildly odoriferous	Odorless	
Number of wipes	Another roll, please!	More than one	One (no stool on paper)	
Post-poo sentiment	Woulda, coulda, shoulda	Satisfaction	Poo-phoria	
			TOTAL	

Name: _____

Date: _____ - ___ - ___   Time: ___ : ___ ☐ AM ☐ PM

Duration: _____

Unusual Characteristics: _____

_____

_____

_____

Sketch:

```
┌ ─ ─ ─ ─ ─ ─ ─ ─ ─ ─ ─ ─ ─ ─ ─ ─ ─ ─ ─ ┐
│                                         │
│                                         │
│                                         │
│                                         │
│                                         │
│                                         │
│                                         │
│                                         │
│                                         │
│                                         │
│                                         │
└ ─ ─ ─ ─ ─ ─ ─ ─ ─ ─ ─ ─ ─ ─ ─ ─ ─ ─ ─ ┘
```

Doo You Know? A recent study showed that, while 95 percent of men and women surveyed say they wash their hands after using a public restroom, only 67 percent of people actually do.

Poo Quality Index (PQI):

	1	2	3	Score
Delivery	Epidural, please!	Couple of pushes, no grunts	Smooth like butter, baby	
Size/Shape	Pebble Poo **OR** Liquid	Snake-like girth **OR** stubby	Monster Poo; stool breaks water surface	
Number of particles	More than two	Two, The Deuce	One and done, baby!	
Smell	Vomit-inducing	Mildly odoriferous	Odorless	
Number of wipes	Another roll, please!	More than one	One (no stool on paper)	
Post-poo sentiment	Woulda, coulda, shoulda	Satisfaction	Poo-phoria	
			TOTAL	

Name: _____

Date: _____ - _____ - _____   Time: _____ : _____ ☐ AM ☐ PM

Duration: _____

Unusual Characteristics: _____

_____

_____

_____

Sketch:

```
┌─────────────────────────────────────┐
│                                     │
│                                     │
│                                     │
│                                     │
│                                     │
│                                     │
│                                     │
└─────────────────────────────────────┘
```

Doo You Know? The average person farts ten times per day, resulting in the release of 705 cc of gas into the atmosphere.

Poo Quality Index (PQI):

	1	2	3	Score
Delivery	Epidural, please!	Couple of pushes, no grunts	Smooth like butter, baby	
Size/Shape	Pebble Poo **OR** Liquid	Snake-like girth **OR** stubby	Monster Poo; stool breaks water surface	
Number of particles	More than two	Two, The Deuce	One and done, baby!	
Smell	Vomit-inducing	Mildly odoriferous	Odorless	
Number of wipes	Another roll, please!	More than one	One (no stool on paper)	
Post-poo sentiment	Woulda, coulda, shoulda	Satisfaction	Poo-phoria	
			TOTAL	

Name: _____

Date: _____ - _____ - _____   Time: _____ : _____ ☐ AM ☐ PM

Duration: _____

Unusual Characteristics: _____

_____

_____

_____

Sketch:

Doo You Know? The average weight of stool excreted per day is 450 grams (about a pound).

Poo Quality Index (PQI):

	1	2	3	Score
Delivery	Epidural, please!	Couple of pushes, no grunts	Smooth like butter, baby	
Size/Shape	Pebble Poo **OR** Liquid	Snake-like girth **OR** stubby	Monster Poo; stool breaks water surface	
Number of particles	More than two	Two, The Deuce	One and done, baby!	
Smell	Vomit-inducing	Mildly odoriferous	Odorless	
Number of wipes	Another roll, please!	More than one	One (no stool on paper)	
Post-poo sentiment	Woulda, coulda, shoulda	Satisfaction	Poo-phoria	
			TOTAL	

Name: _____

Date: _____ - _____ - _____   Time: _____ : _____ ☐ AM ☐ PM

Duration: _____

Unusual Characteristics: _____

_____

_____

_____

Sketch:

Doo You Know? The amount of stool expelled per day varies from country to country. The average weight of stool in England is 106 grams/day, while South Asians unload nearly three times that amount. This difference is largely due to the higher fiber content in the average Indian diet.

Poo Quality Index (PQI):

	1	2	3	Score
Delivery	Epidural, please!	Couple of pushes, no grunts	Smooth like butter, baby	
Size/Shape	Pebble Poo **OR** Liquid	Snake-like girth **OR** stubby	Monster Poo; stool breaks water surface	
Number of particles	More than two	Two, The Deuce	One and done, baby!	
Smell	Vomit-inducing	Mildly odoriferous	Odorless	
Number of wipes	Another roll, please!	More than one	One (no stool on paper)	
Post-poo sentiment	Woulda, coulda, shoulda	Satisfaction	Poo-phoria	
			TOTAL	

Name: _____

Date: _____ - ___ - ___   Time: ___ : ___ ☐ AM ☐ PM

Duration: _____

Unusual Characteristics: _____

_____

_____

_____

Sketch:

Doo You Know? Studies of healthy subjects have revealed a wide variation in stool frequency. The current accepted range for "normal" is from three bowel movements per day to three bowel movements per week.

Poo Quality Index (PQI):

	1	2	3	Score
Delivery	Epidural, please!	Couple of pushes, no grunts	Smooth like butter, baby	
Size/Shape	Pebble Poo **OR** Liquid	Snake-like girth **OR** stubby	Monster Poo; stool breaks water surface	
Number of particles	More than two	Two, The Deuce	One and done, baby!	
Smell	Vomit-inducing	Mildly odoriferous	Odorless	
Number of wipes	Another roll, please!	More than one	One (no stool on paper)	
Post-poo sentiment	Woulda, coulda, shoulda	Satisfaction	Poo-phoria	
			TOTAL	

Name: _____

Date: _____ - _____ - _____   Time: _____ : _____ ☐ AM ☐ PM

Duration: _____

Unusual Characteristics: _____

_____

_____

_____

Sketch:

```
┌ ─ ─ ─ ─ ─ ─ ─ ─ ─ ─ ─ ─ ─ ─ ─ ─ ─ ─ ─ ┐
│                                         │
│                                         │
│                                         │
│                                         │
│                                         │
│                                         │
│                                         │
│                                         │
│                                         │
│                                         │
└ ─ ─ ─ ─ ─ ─ ─ ─ ─ ─ ─ ─ ─ ─ ─ ─ ─ ─ ─ ┘
```

Doo You Know? What's Poo Made Of? •10 parts water •1 part bacteria (dead and alive) •1 part indigestible fiber •1 part mixture of fat, protein, dead cells, mucus

Poo Quality Index (PQI):

	1	2	3	Score
Delivery	Epidural, please!	Couple of pushes, no grunts	Smooth like butter, baby	
Size/Shape	Pebble Poo **OR** Liquid	Snake-like girth **OR** stubby	Monster Poo; stool breaks water surface	
Number of particles	More than two	Two, The Deuce	One and done, baby!	
Smell	Vomit-inducing	Mildly odoriferous	Odorless	
Number of wipes	Another roll, please!	More than one	One (no stool on paper)	
Post-poo sentiment	Woulda, coulda, shoulda	Satisfaction	Poo-phoria	
			TOTAL	

Name: _____

Date: _____ - _____ - _____   Time: _____ : _____ ☐ AM ☐ PM

Duration: _____

Unusual Characteristics: _____

_____

_____

_____

Sketch:

Doo You Know? •Rabbits can produce over 500 pellets of poo every day. •Horses poo ten pounds worth of dung, often without breaking stride. •Geese poo, on average, once every twelve minutes. •Bears don't poo at all when hibernating. Their bodies create an internal plug made from feces and hair that prevents them from pooping while sleeping.

Poo Quality Index (PQI):

	1	2	3	Score
Delivery	Epidural, please!	Couple of pushes, no grunts	Smooth like butter, baby	
Size/Shape	Pebble Poo **OR** Liquid	Snake-like girth **OR** stubby	Monster Poo; stool breaks water surface	
Number of particles	More than two	Two, The Deuce	One and done, baby!	
Smell	Vomit-inducing	Mildly odoriferous	Odorless	
Number of wipes	Another roll, please!	More than one	One (no stool on paper)	
Post-poo sentiment	Woulda, coulda, shoulda	Satisfaction	Poo-phoria	
			TOTAL	

Name:

Date: - -

Time: :   ☐ AM ☐ PM

Duration:

Unusual Characteristics:

Sketch:

Doo You Know? **Foods That Cause Gas:** •Beans •Vegetables, such as broccoli, cabbage, brussels sprouts, onions, artichokes, and asparagus •Fruits, such as pears, apples, and peaches •Whole grains •Soft drinks •Milk •Sorbitol (used as a sugar substitute in diet foods

Poo Quality Index (PQI):

	1	2	3	Score
Delivery	Epidural, please!	Couple of pushes, no grunts	Smooth like butter, baby	
Size/Shape	Pebble Poo **OR** Liquid	Snake-like girth **OR** stubby	Monster Poo; stool breaks water surface	
Number of particles	More than two	Two, The Deuce	One and done, baby!	
Smell	Vomit-inducing	Mildly odoriferous	Odorless	
Number of wipes	Another roll, please!	More than one	One (no stool on paper)	
Post-poo sentiment	Woulda, coulda, shoulda	Satisfaction	Poo-phoria	
			TOTAL	

Name: _____

Date: _____ - __ - __   Time: ___ : __ ☐ AM ☐ PM

Duration: _____

Unusual Characteristics: _____

_____

_____

_____

Sketch:

Doo You Know? A recent study showed that, while 95 percent of men and women surveyed say they wash their hands after using a public restroom, only 67 percent of people actually do.

Poo Quality Index (PQI):

	1	2	3	Score
Delivery	Epidural, please!	Couple of pushes, no grunts	Smooth like butter, baby	
Size/Shape	Pebble Poo **OR** Liquid	Snake-like girth **OR** stubby	Monster Poo; stool breaks water surface	
Number of particles	More than two	Two, The Deuce	One and done, baby!	
Smell	Vomit-inducing	Mildly odoriferous	Odorless	
Number of wipes	Another roll, please!	More than one	One (no stool on paper)	
Post-poo sentiment	Woulda, coulda, shoulda	Satisfaction	Poo-phoria	
			TOTAL	

Name: _____

Date: _____ - __ - __   Time: ____ : ___ ☐ AM ☐ PM

Duration: _____

Unusual Characteristics: _____

_____

_____

_____

Sketch:

```
┌ ─ ─ ─ ─ ─ ─ ─ ─ ─ ─ ─ ─ ─ ─ ─ ─ ─ ─ ─ ─ ─ ┐
│                                           │
│                                           │
│                                           │
│                                           │
│                                           │
│                                           │
│                                           │
│                                           │
│                                           │
└ ─ ─ ─ ─ ─ ─ ─ ─ ─ ─ ─ ─ ─ ─ ─ ─ ─ ─ ─ ─ ─ ┘
```

Doo You Know? The average person farts ten times per day, resulting in the release of 705 cc of gas into the atmosphere.

Poo Quality Index (PQI):

	1	2	3	Score
Delivery	Epidural, please!	Couple of pushes, no grunts	Smooth like butter, baby	
Size/Shape	Pebble Poo **OR** Liquid	Snake-like girth **OR** stubby	Monster Poo; stool breaks water surface	
Number of particles	More than two	Two, The Deuce	One and done, baby!	
Smell	Vomit-inducing	Mildly odoriferous	Odorless	
Number of wipes	Another roll, please!	More than one	One (no stool on paper)	
Post-poo sentiment	Woulda, coulda, shoulda	Satisfaction	Poo-phoria	
			TOTAL	

Name: _____

Date: ____ - ____ - ____   Time: ____ : ____ ☐ AM ☐ PM

Duration: _____

Unusual Characteristics: _____

_____

_____

_____

Sketch:

```
┌ ─ ─ ─ ─ ─ ─ ─ ─ ─ ─ ─ ─ ─ ─ ─ ─ ─ ─ ─ ─ ─ ┐
│                                             │
│                                             │
│                                             │
│                                             │
│                                             │
│                                             │
│                                             │
│                                             │
│                                             │
└ ─ ─ ─ ─ ─ ─ ─ ─ ─ ─ ─ ─ ─ ─ ─ ─ ─ ─ ─ ─ ─ ┘
```

Doo You Know? The average weight of stool excreted per day is 450 grams (about a pound).

Poo Quality Index (PQI):

	1	2	3	Score
Delivery	Epidural, please!	Couple of pushes, no grunts	Smooth like butter, baby	
Size/Shape	Pebble Poo **OR** Liquid	Snake-like girth **OR** stubby	Monster Poo; stool breaks water surface	
Number of particles	More than two	Two, The Deuce	One and done, baby!	
Smell	Vomit-inducing	Mildly odoriferous	Odorless	
Number of wipes	Another roll, please!	More than one	One (no stool on paper)	
Post-poo sentiment	Woulda, coulda, shoulda	Satisfaction	Poo-phoria	
			TOTAL	

Name: _____

Date: ___ - ___ - ___   Time: ___ : ___ ☐ AM ☐ PM

Duration: _____

Unusual Characteristics: _____

_____

_____

_____

Sketch:

```
┌ ─ ─ ─ ─ ─ ─ ─ ─ ─ ─ ─ ─ ─ ─ ─ ─ ─ ─ ┐
│                                      │
│                                      │
│                                      │
│                                      │
│                                      │
│                                      │
│                                      │
│                                      │
│                                      │
│                                      │
│                                      │
└ ─ ─ ─ ─ ─ ─ ─ ─ ─ ─ ─ ─ ─ ─ ─ ─ ─ ─ ┘
```

Doo You Know? The amount of stool expelled per day varies from country to country. The average weight of stool in England is 106 grams/day, while South Asians unload nearly three times that amount. This difference is largely due to the higher fiber content in the average Indian diet.

Poo Quality Index (PQI):

	1	2	3	Score
Delivery	Epidural, please!	Couple of pushes, no grunts	Smooth like butter, baby	
Size/Shape	Pebble Poo **OR** Liquid	Snake-like girth **OR** stubby	Monster Poo; stool breaks water surface	
Number of particles	More than two	Two, The Deuce	One and done, baby!	
Smell	Vomit-inducing	Mildly odoriferous	Odorless	
Number of wipes	Another roll, please!	More than one	One (no stool on paper)	
Post-poo sentiment	Woulda, coulda, shoulda	Satisfaction	Poo-phoria	
			TOTAL	

Name: _____

Date: ___ - ___ - ___   Time: ___ : ___ ☐ AM ☐ PM

Duration: _____

Unusual Characteristics: _____

_____

_____

_____

Sketch:

```
┌ ─ ─ ─ ─ ─ ─ ─ ─ ─ ─ ─ ─ ─ ─ ─ ─ ─ ─ ─ ─ ─ ─ ─ ┐
│                                                 │
│                                                 │
│                                                 │
│                                                 │
│                                                 │
│                                                 │
│                                                 │
│                                                 │
│                                                 │
│                                                 │
└ ─ ─ ─ ─ ─ ─ ─ ─ ─ ─ ─ ─ ─ ─ ─ ─ ─ ─ ─ ─ ─ ─ ─ ┘
```

Doo You Know? Studies of healthy subjects have revealed a wide variation in stool frequency. The current accepted range for "normal" is from three bowel movements per day to three bowel movements per week.

Poo Quality Index (PQI):

	1	2	3	Score
Delivery	Epidural, please!	Couple of pushes, no grunts	Smooth like butter, baby	
Size/Shape	Pebble Poo **OR** Liquid	Snake-like girth **OR** stubby	Monster Poo; stool breaks water surface	
Number of particles	More than two	Two, The Deuce	One and done, baby!	
Smell	Vomit-inducing	Mildly odoriferous	Odorless	
Number of wipes	Another roll, please!	More than one	One (no stool on paper)	
Post-poo sentiment	Woulda, coulda, shoulda	Satisfaction	Poo-phoria	
			TOTAL	

Name: _____

Date: _____ - ___ - ___   Time: ____ : ___ ☐ AM ☐ PM

Duration: _____

Unusual Characteristics: _____

_____

_____

_____

Sketch:

```
┌─────────────────────────────────────────────┐
│                                               │
│                                               │
│                                               │
│                                               │
│                                               │
│                                               │
│                                               │
│                                               │
│                                               │
└─────────────────────────────────────────────┘
```

Doo You Know? **What's Poo Made Of?** •10 parts water •1 part bacteria (dead and alive) •1 part indigestible fiber •1 part mixture of fat, protein, dead cells, mucus

Poo Quality Index (PQI):

	1	2	3	Score
Delivery	Epidural, please!	Couple of pushes, no grunts	Smooth like butter, baby	
Size/Shape	Pebble Poo **OR** Liquid	Snake-like girth **OR** stubby	Monster Poo; stool breaks water surface	
Number of particles	More than two	Two, The Deuce	One and done, baby!	
Smell	Vomit-inducing	Mildly odoriferous	Odorless	
Number of wipes	Another roll, please!	More than one	One (no stool on paper)	
Post-poo sentiment	Woulda, coulda, shoulda	Satisfaction	Poo-phoria	
			TOTAL	

Name: _____

Date: _____ - ___ - ___   Time: _____ : ___ ☐ AM ☐ PM

Duration: _____

Unusual Characteristics: _____

_____

_____

_____

Sketch:

```
┌ ─ ─ ─ ─ ─ ─ ─ ─ ─ ─ ─ ─ ─ ─ ─ ─ ─ ─ ─ ─ ─ ─ ─ ┐
│                                                 │
│                                                 │
│                                                 │
│                                                 │
│                                                 │
│                                                 │
│                                                 │
│                                                 │
│                                                 │
│                                                 │
└ ─ ─ ─ ─ ─ ─ ─ ─ ─ ─ ─ ─ ─ ─ ─ ─ ─ ─ ─ ─ ─ ─ ─ ┘
```

Doo You Know? •Rabbits can produce over 500 pellets of poo every day. •Horses poo ten pounds worth of dung, often without breaking stride. •Geese poo, on average, once every twelve minutes. •Bears don't poo at all when hibernating. Their bodies create an internal plug made from feces and hair that prevents them from pooping while sleeping.

Poo Quality Index (PQI):

	1	2	3	Score
Delivery	Epidural, please!	Couple of pushes, no grunts	Smooth like butter, baby	
Size/Shape	Pebble Poo **OR** Liquid	Snake-like girth **OR** stubby	Monster Poo; stool breaks water surface	
Number of particles	More than two	Two, The Deuce	One and done, baby!	
Smell	Vomit-inducing	Mildly odoriferous	Odorless	
Number of wipes	Another roll, please!	More than one	One (no stool on paper)	
Post-poo sentiment	Woulda, coulda, shoulda	Satisfaction	Poo-phoria	
			TOTAL	

Name: _____

Date: _____ - _____ - _____   Time: _____ : _____ ☐ AM ☐ PM

Duration: _____

Unusual Characteristics: _____

_____

_____

_____

Sketch:

```
┌ ─ ─ ─ ─ ─ ─ ─ ─ ─ ─ ─ ─ ─ ─ ─ ─ ─ ─ ─ ─ ─ ─ ─ ┐
│                                                 │
│                                                 │
│                                                 │
│                                                 │
│                                                 │
│                                                 │
│                                                 │
│                                                 │
│                                                 │
│                                                 │
└ ─ ─ ─ ─ ─ ─ ─ ─ ─ ─ ─ ─ ─ ─ ─ ─ ─ ─ ─ ─ ─ ─ ─ ┘
```

Doo You Know? **Foods That Cause Gas:** •Beans •Vegetables, such as broccoli, cabbage, brussels sprouts, onions, artichokes, and asparagus •Fruits, such as pears, apples, and peaches •Whole grains •Soft drinks •Milk •Sorbitol (used as a sugar substitute in diet foods

Poo Quality Index (PQI):

	1	2	3	Score
Delivery	Epidural, please!	Couple of pushes, no grunts	Smooth like butter, baby	
Size/Shape	Pebble Poo **OR** Liquid	Snake-like girth **OR** stubby	Monster Poo; stool breaks water surface	
Number of particles	More than two	Two, The Deuce	One and done, baby!	
Smell	Vomit-inducing	Mildly odoriferous	Odorless	
Number of wipes	Another roll, please!	More than one	One (no stool on paper)	
Post-poo sentiment	Woulda, coulda, shoulda	Satisfaction	Poo-phoria	
			TOTAL	

Name:

Date: -   -   Time: :   ☐ AM ☐ PM

Duration:

Unusual Characteristics:

Sketch:

Doo You Know? A recent study showed that, while 95 percent of men and women surveyed say they wash their hands after using a public restroom, only 67 percent of people actually do.

Poo Quality Index (PQI):

	1	2	3	Score
Delivery	Epidural, please!	Couple of pushes, no grunts	Smooth like butter, baby	
Size/Shape	Pebble Poo **OR** Liquid	Snake-like girth **OR** stubby	Monster Poo; stool breaks water surface	
Number of particles	More than two	Two, The Deuce	One and done, baby!	
Smell	Vomit-inducing	Mildly odoriferous	Odorless	
Number of wipes	Another roll, please!	More than one	One (no stool on paper)	
Post-poo sentiment	Woulda, coulda, shoulda	Satisfaction	Poo-phoria	
			TOTAL	

Name: _____

Date: _____ - ___ - ___   Time: ____ : ____ ☐ AM ☐ PM

Duration: _____

Unusual Characteristics: _____

_____

_____

_____

Sketch:

Doo You Know? The average person farts ten times per day, resulting in the release of 705 cc of gas into the atmosphere.

Poo Quality Index (PQI):

	1	2	3	Score
Delivery	Epidural, please!	Couple of pushes, no grunts	Smooth like butter, baby	
Size/Shape	Pebble Poo **OR** Liquid	Snake-like girth **OR** stubby	Monster Poo; stool breaks water surface	
Number of particles	More than two	Two, The Deuce	One and done, baby!	
Smell	Vomit-inducing	Mildly odoriferous	Odorless	
Number of wipes	Another roll, please!	More than one	One (no stool on paper)	
Post-poo sentiment	Woulda, coulda, shoulda	Satisfaction	Poo-phoria	
			TOTAL	

Name: _____

Date: ___ - ___ - ___   Time: ___ : ___ ☐ AM ☐ PM

Duration: _____

Unusual Characteristics: _____

_____

_____

_____

Sketch:

```
┌ ─ ─ ─ ─ ─ ─ ─ ─ ─ ─ ─ ─ ─ ─ ─ ─ ─ ─ ─ ─ ┐
│                                          │
│                                          │
│                                          │
│                                          │
│                                          │
│                                          │
│                                          │
│                                          │
│                                          │
└ ─ ─ ─ ─ ─ ─ ─ ─ ─ ─ ─ ─ ─ ─ ─ ─ ─ ─ ─ ─ ┘
```

Doo You Know? The average weight of stool excreted per day is 450 grams (about a pound).

Poo Quality Index (PQI):

	1	2	3	Score
Delivery	Epidural, please!	Couple of pushes, no grunts	Smooth like butter, baby	
Size/Shape	Pebble Poo **OR** Liquid	Snake-like girth **OR** stubby	Monster Poo; stool breaks water surface	
Number of particles	More than two	Two, The Deuce	One and done, baby!	
Smell	Vomit-inducing	Mildly odoriferous	Odorless	
Number of wipes	Another roll, please!	More than one	One (no stool on paper)	
Post-poo sentiment	Woulda, coulda, shoulda	Satisfaction	Poo-phoria	
			TOTAL	

Name: _____

Date: _____ - ___ - ___   Time: _____ : ___ ☐ AM ☐ PM

Duration: _____

Unusual Characteristics: _____

_____

_____

_____

Sketch:

```
┌─────────────────────────────────────────────┐
│                                               │
│                                               │
│                                               │
│                                               │
│                                               │
│                                               │
│                                               │
│                                               │
│                                               │
│                                               │
└─────────────────────────────────────────────┘
```

Doo You Know? The amount of stool expelled per day varies from country to country. The average weight of stool in England is 106 grams/day, while South Asians unload nearly three times that amount. This difference is largely due to the higher fiber content in the average Indian diet.

Poo Quality Index (PQI):

	1	2	3	Score
Delivery	Epidural, please!	Couple of pushes, no grunts	Smooth like butter, baby	
Size/Shape	Pebble Poo **OR** Liquid	Snake-like girth **OR** stubby	Monster Poo; stool breaks water surface	
Number of particles	More than two	Two, The Deuce	One and done, baby!	
Smell	Vomit-inducing	Mildly odoriferous	Odorless	
Number of wipes	Another roll, please!	More than one	One (no stool on paper)	
Post-poo sentiment	Woulda, coulda, shoulda	Satisfaction	Poo-phoria	
			TOTAL	

Name: _____

Date: ____ - ____ - ____   **Time:** ____ : ____ ☐ AM ☐ PM

Duration: _____

Unusual Characteristics: _____

_____

_____

_____

Sketch:

Doo You Know? Studies of healthy subjects have revealed a wide variation in stool frequency. The current accepted range for "normal" is from three bowel movements per day to three bowel movements per week.

Poo Quality Index (PQI):

	1	2	3	Score
Delivery	Epidural, please!	Couple of pushes, no grunts	Smooth like butter, baby	
Size/Shape	Pebble Poo **OR** Liquid	Snake-like girth **OR** stubby	Monster Poo; stool breaks water surface	
Number of particles	More than two	Two, The Deuce	One and done, baby!	
Smell	Vomit-inducing	Mildly odoriferous	Odorless	
Number of wipes	Another roll, please!	More than one	One (no stool on paper)	
Post-poo sentiment	Woulda, coulda, shoulda	Satisfaction	Poo-phoria	
			TOTAL	

Name: _____

Date: _____ - _____ - _____   Time: _____ : _____ ☐ AM ☐ PM

Duration: _____

Unusual Characteristics: _____

_____

_____

_____

Sketch:

```
┌ ─ ─ ─ ─ ─ ─ ─ ─ ─ ─ ─ ─ ─ ─ ─ ─ ┐
│                                 │
│                                 │
│                                 │
│                                 │
│                                 │
│                                 │
│                                 │
│                                 │
│                                 │
│                                 │
└ ─ ─ ─ ─ ─ ─ ─ ─ ─ ─ ─ ─ ─ ─ ─ ─ ┘
```

Doo You Know? What's Poo Made Of? •10 parts water •1 part bacteria (dead and alive) •1 part indigestible fiber •1 part mixture of fat, protein, dead cells, mucus

Poo Quality Index (PQI):

	1	2	3	Score
Delivery	Epidural, please!	Couple of pushes, no grunts	Smooth like butter, baby	
Size/Shape	Pebble Poo **OR** Liquid	Snake-like girth **OR** stubby	Monster Poo; stool breaks water surface	
Number of particles	More than two	Two, The Deuce	One and done, baby!	
Smell	Vomit-inducing	Mildly odoriferous	Odorless	
Number of wipes	Another roll, please!	More than one	One (no stool on paper)	
Post-poo sentiment	Woulda, coulda, shoulda	Satisfaction	Poo-phoria	
			TOTAL	

Name:

Date: -   -   Time: :   ☐ AM ☐ PM

Duration:

Unusual Characteristics:

Sketch:

Doo You Know? •Rabbits can produce over 500 pellets of poo every day. •Horses poo ten pounds worth of dung, often without breaking stride. •Geese poo, on average, once every twelve minutes. •Bears don't poo at all when hibernating. Their bodies create an internal plug made from feces and hair that prevents them from pooping while sleeping.

Poo Quality Index (PQI):

	1	2	3	Score
Delivery	Epidural, please!	Couple of pushes, no grunts	Smooth like butter, baby	
Size/Shape	Pebble Poo **OR** Liquid	Snake-like girth **OR** stubby	Monster Poo; stool breaks water surface	
Number of particles	More than two	Two, The Deuce	One and done, baby!	
Smell	Vomit-inducing	Mildly odoriferous	Odorless	
Number of wipes	Another roll, please!	More than one	One (no stool on paper)	
Post-poo sentiment	Woulda, coulda, shoulda	Satisfaction	Poo-phoria	
			TOTAL	

Name: _____

Date: _____ - _____ - _____   Time: _____ : _____ ☐ AM ☐ PM

Duration: _____

Unusual Characteristics: _____

_____

_____

_____

Sketch:

┌───┐
│   │
│   │
│   │
│   │
│   │
│   │
│   │
│   │
│   │
└───┘

Doo You Know? **Foods That Cause Gas:** •Beans •Vegetables, such as broccoli, cabbage, brussels sprouts, onions, artichokes, and asparagus •Fruits, such as pears, apples, and peaches •Whole grains •Soft drinks •Milk •Sorbitol (used as a sugar substitute in diet foods

Poo Quality Index (PQI):

	1	2	3	Score
Delivery	Epidural, please!	Couple of pushes, no grunts	Smooth like butter, baby	
Size/Shape	Pebble Poo **OR** Liquid	Snake-like girth **OR** stubby	Monster Poo; stool breaks water surface	
Number of particles	More than two	Two, The Deuce	One and done, baby!	
Smell	Vomit-inducing	Mildly odoriferous	Odorless	
Number of wipes	Another roll, please!	More than one	One (no stool on paper)	
Post-poo sentiment	Woulda, coulda, shoulda	Satisfaction	Poo-phoria	
			TOTAL	

Name: _____

Date: _____ - _____ - _____   Time: _____ : _____ ☐ AM ☐ PM

Duration: _____

Unusual Characteristics: _____

_____

_____

_____

Sketch:

```
┌ ─ ─ ─ ─ ─ ─ ─ ─ ─ ─ ─ ─ ─ ─ ─ ─ ─ ─ ─ ─ ─ ┐
│                                             │
│                                             │
│                                             │
│                                             │
│                                             │
│                                             │
│                                             │
│                                             │
│                                             │
│                                             │
│                                             │
└ ─ ─ ─ ─ ─ ─ ─ ─ ─ ─ ─ ─ ─ ─ ─ ─ ─ ─ ─ ─ ─ ┘
```

Doo You Know? A recent study showed that, while 95 percent of men and women surveyed say they wash their hands after using a public restroom, only 67 percent of people actually do.

Poo Quality Index (PQI):

	1	2	3	Score
Delivery	Epidural, please!	Couple of pushes, no grunts	Smooth like butter, baby	
Size/Shape	Pebble Poo **OR** Liquid	Snake-like girth **OR** stubby	Monster Poo; stool breaks water surface	
Number of particles	More than two	Two, The Deuce	One and done, baby!	
Smell	Vomit-inducing	Mildly odoriferous	Odorless	
Number of wipes	Another roll, please!	More than one	One (no stool on paper)	
Post-poo sentiment	Woulda, coulda, shoulda	Satisfaction	Poo-phoria	
			TOTAL	

Name: _____

Date: _____ - ___ - ___   Time: ___ : ___ ☐ AM ☐ PM

Duration: _____

Unusual Characteristics: _____

_____

_____

_____

Sketch:

```
┌ ─ ─ ─ ─ ─ ─ ─ ─ ─ ─ ─ ─ ─ ─ ─ ─ ─ ─ ─ ─ ─ ┐
│                                           │
│                                           │
│                                           │
│                                           │
│                                           │
│                                           │
│                                           │
│                                           │
└ ─ ─ ─ ─ ─ ─ ─ ─ ─ ─ ─ ─ ─ ─ ─ ─ ─ ─ ─ ─ ─ ┘
```

Doo You Know? The average person farts ten times per day, resulting in the release of 705 cc of gas into the atmosphere.

Poo Quality Index (PQI):

	1	2	3	Score
Delivery	Epidural, please!	Couple of pushes, no grunts	Smooth like butter, baby	
Size/Shape	Pebble Poo **OR** Liquid	Snake-like girth **OR** stubby	Monster Poo; stool breaks water surface	
Number of particles	More than two	Two, The Deuce	One and done, baby!	
Smell	Vomit-inducing	Mildly odoriferous	Odorless	
Number of wipes	Another roll, please!	More than one	One (no stool on paper)	
Post-poo sentiment	Woulda, coulda, shoulda	Satisfaction	Poo-phoria	
			TOTAL	

Name:

Date: -   -

Time: :   ☐ AM ☐ PM

Duration:

Unusual Characteristics:

Sketch:

Doo You Know? The average weight of stool excreted per day is 450 grams (about a pound).

Poo Quality Index (PQI):

	1	2	3	Score
Delivery	Epidural, please!	Couple of pushes, no grunts	Smooth like butter, baby	
Size/Shape	Pebble Poo **OR** Liquid	Snake-like girth **OR** stubby	Monster Poo; stool breaks water surface	
Number of particles	More than two	Two, The Deuce	One and done, baby!	
Smell	Vomit-inducing	Mildly odoriferous	Odorless	
Number of wipes	Another roll, please!	More than one	One (no stool on paper)	
Post-poo sentiment	Woulda, coulda, shoulda	Satisfaction	Poo-phoria	
			TOTAL	

Name: _____

Date: _____ - ____ - ____   Time: ____ : ____ ☐ AM ☐ PM

Duration: _____

Unusual Characteristics: _____

_____

_____

_____

Sketch:

┌───┐
│   │
│   │
│   │
│   │
│   │
│   │
│   │
│   │
│   │
│   │
└───┘

Doo You Know? The amount of stool expelled per day varies from country to country. The average weight of stool in England is 106 grams/day, while South Asians unload nearly three times that amount. This difference is largely due to the higher fiber content in the average Indian diet.

Poo Quality Index (PQI):

	1	2	3	Score
Delivery	Epidural, please!	Couple of pushes, no grunts	Smooth like butter, baby	
Size/Shape	Pebble Poo **OR** Liquid	Snake-like girth **OR** stubby	Monster Poo; stool breaks water surface	
Number of particles	More than two	Two, The Deuce	One and done, baby!	
Smell	Vomit-inducing	Mildly odoriferous	Odorless	
Number of wipes	Another roll, please!	More than one	One (no stool on paper)	
Post-poo sentiment	Woulda, coulda, shoulda	Satisfaction	Poo-phoria	
			TOTAL	

Name: _____

Date: _____ - _____ - _____   Time: _____ : _____ ☐ AM ☐ PM

Duration: _____

Unusual Characteristics: _____

_____

_____

_____

Sketch:

```
┌ ─ ─ ─ ─ ─ ─ ─ ─ ─ ─ ─ ─ ─ ─ ─ ─ ─ ─ ─ ─ ─ ─ ─ ─ ┐
│                                                   │
│                                                   │
│                                                   │
│                                                   │
│                                                   │
│                                                   │
│                                                   │
│                                                   │
│                                                   │
└ ─ ─ ─ ─ ─ ─ ─ ─ ─ ─ ─ ─ ─ ─ ─ ─ ─ ─ ─ ─ ─ ─ ─ ─ ┘
```

Doo You Know? Studies of healthy subjects have revealed a wide variation in stool frequency. The current accepted range for "normal" is from three bowel movements per day to three bowel movements per week.

Poo Quality Index (PQI):

	1	2	3	Score
Delivery	Epidural, please!	Couple of pushes, no grunts	Smooth like butter, baby	
Size/Shape	Pebble Poo **OR** Liquid	Snake-like girth **OR** stubby	Monster Poo; stool breaks water surface	
Number of particles	More than two	Two, The Deuce	One and done, baby!	
Smell	Vomit-inducing	Mildly odoriferous	Odorless	
Number of wipes	Another roll, please!	More than one	One (no stool on paper)	
Post-poo sentiment	Woulda, coulda, shoulda	Satisfaction	Poo-phoria	
			TOTAL	

Name: _____

Date: ____ - ___ - ___   Time: ____ : ____ ☐AM ☐PM

Duration: _____

Unusual Characteristics: _____

_____

_____

_____

Sketch:

```
┌ ─ ─ ─ ─ ─ ─ ─ ─ ─ ─ ─ ─ ─ ─ ─ ─ ─ ─ ─ ┐
│                                        │
│                                        │
│                                        │
│                                        │
│                                        │
│                                        │
│                                        │
│                                        │
│                                        │
│                                        │
└ ─ ─ ─ ─ ─ ─ ─ ─ ─ ─ ─ ─ ─ ─ ─ ─ ─ ─ ─ ┘
```

Doo You Know? **What's Poo Made Of?** •10 parts water •1 part bacteria (dead and alive) •1 part indigestible fiber •1 part mixture of fat, protein, dead cells, mucus

Poo Quality Index (PQI):

	1	2	3	Score
Delivery	Epidural, please!	Couple of pushes, no grunts	Smooth like butter, baby	
Size/Shape	Pebble Poo **OR** Liquid	Snake-like girth **OR** stubby	Monster Poo; stool breaks water surface	
Number of particles	More than two	Two, The Deuce	One and done, baby!	
Smell	Vomit-inducing	Mildly odoriferous	Odorless	
Number of wipes	Another roll, please!	More than one	One (no stool on paper)	
Post-poo sentiment	Woulda, coulda, shoulda	Satisfaction	Poo-phoria	
			TOTAL	

Name: _____

Date: _____ - _____ - _____   Time: _____ : _____ ☐ AM ☐ PM

Duration: _____

Unusual Characteristics: _____

_____

_____

_____

Sketch:

```
┌─────────────────────────────────────────┐
│                                         │
│                                         │
│                                         │
│                                         │
│                                         │
│                                         │
│                                         │
│                                         │
│                                         │
│                                         │
└─────────────────────────────────────────┘
```

Doo You Know? •Rabbits can produce over 500 pellets of poo every day. •Horses poo ten pounds worth of dung, often without breaking stride. •Geese poo, on average, once every twelve minutes. •Bears don't poo at all when hibernating. Their bodies create an internal plug made from feces and hair that prevents them from pooping while sleeping.

Poo Quality Index (PQI):

	1	2	3	Score
Delivery	Epidural, please!	Couple of pushes, no grunts	Smooth like butter, baby	
Size/Shape	Pebble Poo **OR** Liquid	Snake-like girth **OR** stubby	Monster Poo; stool breaks water surface	
Number of particles	More than two	Two, The Deuce	One and done, baby!	
Smell	Vomit-inducing	Mildly odoriferous	Odorless	
Number of wipes	Another roll, please!	More than one	One (no stool on paper)	
Post-poo sentiment	Woulda, coulda, shoulda	Satisfaction	Poo-phoria	
			TOTAL	

Name: _____

Date: _____ - ___ - ___   **Time:** ___ : ___ ☐ AM ☐ PM

Duration: _____

Unusual Characteristics: _____

_____

_____

_____

Sketch:

Doo You Know? **Foods That Cause Gas:** •Beans •Vegetables, such as broccoli, cabbage, brussels sprouts, onions, artichokes, and asparagus •Fruits, such as pears, apples, and peaches •Whole grains •Soft drinks •Milk •Sorbitol (used as a sugar substitute in diet foods

Poo Quality Index (PQI):

	1	2	3	Score
Delivery	Epidural, please!	Couple of pushes, no grunts	Smooth like butter, baby	
Size/Shape	Pebble Poo **OR** Liquid	Snake-like girth **OR** stubby	Monster Poo; stool breaks water surface	
Number of particles	More than two	Two, The Deuce	One and done, baby!	
Smell	Vomit-inducing	Mildly odoriferous	Odorless	
Number of wipes	Another roll, please!	More than one	One (no stool on paper)	
Post-poo sentiment	Woulda, coulda, shoulda	Satisfaction	Poo-phoria	
			TOTAL	

Name: _____

Date: ___ - ___ - ___   Time: ___ : ___ ☐ AM ☐ PM

Duration: _____

Unusual Characteristics: _____

_____

_____

_____

Sketch:

```
┌ ─ ─ ─ ─ ─ ─ ─ ─ ─ ─ ─ ─ ─ ─ ─ ─ ─ ─ ─ ┐
│                                         │
│                                         │
│                                         │
│                                         │
│                                         │
│                                         │
│                                         │
│                                         │
└ ─ ─ ─ ─ ─ ─ ─ ─ ─ ─ ─ ─ ─ ─ ─ ─ ─ ─ ─ ┘
```

Doo You Know? A recent study showed that, while 95 percent of men and women surveyed say they wash their hands after using a public restroom, only 67 percent of people actually do.

Poo Quality Index (PQI):

	1	2	3	Score
Delivery	Epidural, please!	Couple of pushes, no grunts	Smooth like butter, baby	
Size/Shape	Pebble Poo **OR** Liquid	Snake-like girth **OR** stubby	Monster Poo; stool breaks water surface	
Number of particles	More than two	Two, The Deuce	One and done, baby!	
Smell	Vomit-inducing	Mildly odoriferous	Odorless	
Number of wipes	Another roll, please!	More than one	One (no stool on paper)	
Post-poo sentiment	Woulda, coulda, shoulda	Satisfaction	Poo-phoria	
			TOTAL	

Name: _____

Date: _____ - _____ - _____   Time: _____ : _____ ☐ AM ☐ PM

Duration: _____

Unusual Characteristics: _____

_____

_____

_____

Sketch:

```
┌─────────────────────────────────────┐
│                                     │
│                                     │
│                                     │
│                                     │
│                                     │
│                                     │
│                                     │
│                                     │
│                                     │
└─────────────────────────────────────┘
```

Doo You Know? The average person farts ten times per day, resulting in the release of 705 cc of gas into the atmosphere.

Poo Quality Index (PQI):

	1	2	3	Score
Delivery	Epidural, please!	Couple of pushes, no grunts	Smooth like butter, baby	
Size/Shape	Pebble Poo **OR** Liquid	Snake-like girth **OR** stubby	Monster Poo; stool breaks water surface	
Number of particles	More than two	Two, The Deuce	One and done, baby!	
Smell	Vomit-inducing	Mildly odoriferous	Odorless	
Number of wipes	Another roll, please!	More than one	One (no stool on paper)	
Post-poo sentiment	Woulda, coulda, shoulda	Satisfaction	Poo-phoria	
			TOTAL	

Name:

Date: _____ - _____ - _____   Time: _____ : _____ ☐ AM ☐ PM

Duration: _____

Unusual Characteristics: _____

_____

_____

_____

Sketch:

Doo You Know? The average weight of stool excreted per day is 450 grams (about a pound).

Poo Quality Index (PQI):

	1	2	3	Score
Delivery	Epidural, please!	Couple of pushes, no grunts	Smooth like butter, baby	
Size/Shape	Pebble Poo **OR** Liquid	Snake-like girth **OR** stubby	Monster Poo; stool breaks water surface	
Number of particles	More than two	Two, The Deuce	One and done, baby!	
Smell	Vomit-inducing	Mildly odoriferous	Odorless	
Number of wipes	Another roll, please!	More than one	One (no stool on paper)	
Post-poo sentiment	Woulda, coulda, shoulda	Satisfaction	Poo-phoria	
			TOTAL	

Name: _____

Date: _____ - _____ - _____   Time: _____ : _____ ☐ AM ☐ PM

Duration: _____

Unusual Characteristics: _____

_____

_____

_____

Sketch:

```
┌ ─ ─ ─ ─ ─ ─ ─ ─ ─ ─ ─ ─ ─ ─ ─ ─ ─ ─ ┐
│                                      │
│                                      │
│                                      │
│                                      │
│                                      │
│                                      │
│                                      │
│                                      │
│                                      │
│                                      │
└ ─ ─ ─ ─ ─ ─ ─ ─ ─ ─ ─ ─ ─ ─ ─ ─ ─ ─ ┘
```

Doo You Know? Studies of healthy subjects have revealed a wide variation in stool frequency. The current accepted range for "normal" is from three bowel movements per day to three bowel movements per week.

Poo Quality Index (PQI):

	1	2	3	Score
Delivery	Epidural, please!	Couple of pushes, no grunts	Smooth like butter, baby	
Size/Shape	Pebble Poo **OR** Liquid	Snake-like girth **OR** stubby	Monster Poo; stool breaks water surface	
Number of particles	More than two	Two, The Deuce	One and done, baby!	
Smell	Vomit-inducing	Mildly odoriferous	Odorless	
Number of wipes	Another roll, please!	More than one	One (no stool on paper)	
Post-poo sentiment	Woulda, coulda, shoulda	Satisfaction	Poo-phoria	
			TOTAL	

Name: _____

Date: _____ - ___ - ___   Time: _____ : ___ ☐ AM ☐ PM

Duration: _____

Unusual Characteristics: _____

_____

_____

_____

Sketch:

```
┌ ─ ─ ─ ─ ─ ─ ─ ─ ─ ─ ─ ─ ─ ─ ─ ─ ─ ─ ─ ─ ┐
│                                          │
│                                          │
│                                          │
│                                          │
│                                          │
│                                          │
│                                          │
│                                          │
│                                          │
│                                          │
└ ─ ─ ─ ─ ─ ─ ─ ─ ─ ─ ─ ─ ─ ─ ─ ─ ─ ─ ─ ─ ┘
```

Doo You Know? **What's Poo Made Of?** •10 parts water •1 part bacteria (dead and alive) •1 part indigestible fiber •1 part mixture of fat, protein, dead cells, mucus

Poo Quality Index (PQI):

	1	2	3	Score
Delivery	Epidural, please!	Couple of pushes, no grunts	Smooth like butter, baby	
Size/Shape	Pebble Poo **OR** Liquid	Snake-like girth **OR** stubby	Monster Poo; stool breaks water surface	
Number of particles	More than two	Two, The Deuce	One and done, baby!	
Smell	Vomit-inducing	Mildly odoriferous	Odorless	
Number of wipes	Another roll, please!	More than one	One (no stool on paper)	
Post-poo sentiment	Woulda, coulda, shoulda	Satisfaction	Poo-phoria	
			TOTAL	

Name:

Date: - -   Time: : ☐ AM ☐ PM

Duration:

Unusual Characteristics:

Sketch:

Doo You Know? •Rabbits can produce over 500 pellets of poo every day. •Horses poo ten pounds worth of dung, often without breaking stride. •Geese poo, on average, once every twelve minutes. •Bears don't poo at all when hibernating. Their bodies create an internal plug made from feces and hair that prevents them from pooping while sleeping.

Poo Quality Index (PQI):

	1	2	3	Score
Delivery	Epidural, please!	Couple of pushes, no grunts	Smooth like butter, baby	
Size/Shape	Pebble Poo **OR** Liquid	Snake-like girth **OR** stubby	Monster Poo; stool breaks water surface	
Number of particles	More than two	Two, The Deuce	One and done, baby!	
Smell	Vomit-inducing	Mildly odoriferous	Odorless	
Number of wipes	Another roll, please!	More than one	One (no stool on paper)	
Post-poo sentiment	Woulda, coulda, shoulda	Satisfaction	Poo-phoria	
			TOTAL	

Name: _____

Date: _____ - _____ - _____   Time: _____ : _____ ☐ AM ☐ PM

Duration: _____

Unusual Characteristics: _____

_____

_____

_____

Sketch:

```
┌─────────────────────────────────────────────┐
│                                             │
│                                             │
│                                             │
│                                             │
│                                             │
│                                             │
│                                             │
│                                             │
│                                             │
│                                             │
│                                             │
└─────────────────────────────────────────────┘
```

Doo You Know? **Foods That Cause Gas:** •Beans •Vegetables, such as broccoli, cabbage, brussels sprouts, onions, artichokes, and asparagus •Fruits, such as pears, apples, and peaches •Whole grains •Soft drinks •Milk •Sorbitol (used as a sugar substitute in diet foods

Poo Quality Index (PQI):

	1	2	3	Score
Delivery	Epidural, please!	Couple of pushes, no grunts	Smooth like butter, baby	
Size/Shape	Pebble Poo **OR** Liquid	Snake-like girth **OR** stubby	Monster Poo; stool breaks water surface	
Number of particles	More than two	Two, The Deuce	One and done, baby!	
Smell	Vomit-inducing	Mildly odoriferous	Odorless	
Number of wipes	Another roll, please!	More than one	One (no stool on paper)	
Post-poo sentiment	Woulda, coulda, shoulda	Satisfaction	Poo-phoria	
			TOTAL	

Name: _____

Date: ___ - ___ - ___   Time: ___ : ___ ☐ AM ☐ PM

Duration: _____

Unusual Characteristics: _____

_____

_____

_____

Sketch:

```
┌ ─ ─ ─ ─ ─ ─ ─ ─ ─ ─ ─ ─ ─ ─ ─ ─ ─ ─ ─ ─ ─ ┐
│                                            │
│                                            │
│                                            │
│                                            │
│                                            │
│                                            │
│                                            │
│                                            │
│                                            │
│                                            │
└ ─ ─ ─ ─ ─ ─ ─ ─ ─ ─ ─ ─ ─ ─ ─ ─ ─ ─ ─ ─ ─ ┘
```

Doo You Know? A recent study showed that, while 95 percent of men and women surveyed say they wash their hands after using a public restroom, only 67 percent of people actually do.

Poo Quality Index (PQI):

	1	2	3	Score
Delivery	Epidural, please!	Couple of pushes, no grunts	Smooth like butter, baby	
Size/Shape	Pebble Poo **OR** Liquid	Snake-like girth **OR** stubby	Monster Poo; stool breaks water surface	
Number of particles	More than two	Two, The Deuce	One and done, baby!	
Smell	Vomit-inducing	Mildly odoriferous	Odorless	
Number of wipes	Another roll, please!	More than one	One (no stool on paper)	
Post-poo sentiment	Woulda, coulda, shoulda	Satisfaction	Poo-phoria	
			TOTAL	

Name: _____

Date: ___ - ___ - ___   Time: ___ : ___ ☐ AM ☐ PM

Duration: _____

Unusual Characteristics: _____

_____

_____

_____

Sketch:

Doo You Know? The average person farts ten times per day, resulting in the release of 705 cc of gas into the atmosphere.